well, it got 4 stars on tripadvisor

ISBN 978-1-3999-3786-3

Cover designed by Warren Smith & Sam Reynolds
Cover created by Sam Reynolds

Please do get in touch
desperate.measure@outlook.com

desperatesaloon on Instagram

Desperate Measures

Things have been bad
And now they've got worse
Because the final resort
Is this half-arsed verse.

Well, that's just a joke,
So it better be funny,
Cos you need a laugh
And I need the money.

The Last Shot

Outside Work

Softly creeps the builder
Up the scaffold high,
Gone to do his business
Way beyond my eye.

But he's not fixing tiling
In the leaking roof for me.
He's gone to read the paper
And drink a cup of tea.

Barista Blues

I grind the coffee.
I grind my teeth.
Espresso flows.
The cup's beneath.
Oh no, it's not.
Shit! I forgot.
My life's a double-shot latte of grief.

Fast Food

Couldn't be arsed to cook a meal,
Or go out for Sunday dinner.
Got on that app to order in.
Everyone's a winner!

Scooter-man gets some cash.
We get a ready-made roast.
But in a rush, he jumped the lights
And now he's bloody toast.

Do Not Like This

I can see you coming
From here behind the tree.
But I am really bursting,
So it doesn't bother me.

But now you've got your phone out.
That's bad, I won't survive
A global viral piss-take
Now I'm streaming live.

The Way of Yoga

Toes, toes,
Touch your toes,
With your nose.
What other way?
It's yoga!

Back, back,
Bend your back
And bend it back,
Not the other way.
It's yoga!

Face, face,
Make a face.
It fucking hurts.
It's the only way.
It's yoga!

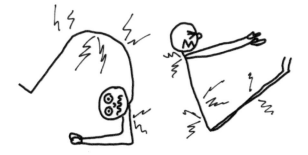

Reality Check

The bank gives you credit
For taking on debt.
You've got a house.
You're a good bet.

You lose your job.
You can't pay the loan.
You're even more screwed.
The bank's got your home.

The Vegan Thief Guild's Motto

Do not fret at checkout.
Be not in a hurry to pay.
Eat your fresh veg in there.
Go at least five times a day.

Pipe Dream

All the time that's wasted,
All the hours spent
Washing dirty dishes
Just to pay the rent.

If I'd know just what was coming
When I had been at school,
I'd not have sneered at plumbing.
Now I'm feeling like a tool.

Open Plan

It's called a floor.
It's got a door
And rows of desks and seating.

There's a cupboard I pass
That's made of glass,
Where people hold a meeting.

There's no fresh air,
Just a whiff of despair.
Head down and hit that keyboard.

It's horrible in here.
Either I head out for a beer
Or hang from the power chord.

The Lark's Song

Hark to the drills of spring.
Us builders have come out.

Making a din's our thing.
We don't mess about!

Listen to the stuff we fling.
Lovin' that smash and clout!

What sweet songs we sing.
FUCK! SHIT! that's what we shout.

Short Cut

Is it a car?
Is it a plane?
Your foot's stuck in tracks.
It's a train.

Here it comes
With a sound like thunder.
The only place you're going
Is six foot under.

Nipping over the rails...
Not a great thought
But it was a short cut
...of a sort.

Reunion

I've just dropped by to say hello.
I know I died a while ago.

Don't grab your heart and go all white.
Just to say - I'm doing all right.

But now I see you're turning blue,
I've been a fright, now you're dead too

But anyway - death will be ok,
Which is what I'd dropped by to say.

It Changed My Life

It said its name was Zircon
And was from outer space.
Its body was a furry ball.
It didn't have a face.

It was looking for a mate here.
I said, "You'll have a wait".
"Not at all," it said, "I've found one."
This was to be my fate.

I laughed but looked in horror
As its tummy twitched and grew
A tentacle that touched me.
Now I'm a fur-ball too.

Natural Instinct

The birds on the tree
Are looking at me.
Oh.
No they're not.

Natural Instinct (Number II)

Watch him go, bounding away,
Into the wind, to bounce and play.
Down to the park for doggie fun.
Hark to the bark - look at him run!

But its not what it seems,
Not even a bit.
He's just desperately keen
To take a big shit.

The Poet

Walking walking walking
Talking talking talking
To myself
All the time
I must be fucking mad

The Poet (Back Again)

At eventide, when night draws near,
As darkness comes, it's time for beer.
Down to the pub, like yesterday,
Or truth be told,
Like lunchtime.

Life Flows Like a River

Fast at first, up keen and bubbly,
Then pushing and weaving
Through soil so thick.

Slow at last, reaching the sea,
Now gasping and wheezing,
Going down like a brick.

Out The Door

Where have the keys gone?
Where is my phone?
I cannot find a fucking thing
In my messy home.

... well, its not here, is it?!

The High Life

It's up his nose
And off he goes,
Life's a great success.
Now in the mood
For fancy food,
Rich pickings of excess.

The end of days
In a dizzy haze,
Heart attack draws near.
Coke is bad
But of the stuff you've had,
It's the brie you need to fear.

Rolling In It

I don't want a lot,
Just what I've got,
Which is quite a bit.
I'm a greedy shit.

Private Member

He's got concrete balls
On the front gate.
He's got a statue of Caesar.
He's not your mate.

He's got a black Merc,
Takes it out for a ride.
It's windows are dark.
No looking inside.

I'm special, he's saying,
But he's not talking to you.
He only hangs with members
Of the Fuck You Crew.

Zen Corner

A series of short, bleak poems using a special oriental technique

What sort of man are you,
Crying over spilt milk?
I am a poor dairy farmer
With only one cow.

The man with many clothes
Who has no wardrobe
Walks a floor of great hazard
And has nowhere to sit.

The road is long.
The path is hard.
There may have been a better way.

All our yesterdays are gone,
Leaving us only with today.
And tomorrow.

I fall strangely down the stairs
Like the swirling leaves in autumn,
But harder.

Night becomes day
But my nightmares
Do not go away.
I start work at dawn.

The uphill road
Will surely go downhill.
Such is the way of life.

In a mood I stew.
Lay no blame on me.
As always,
It is you.

Warm spots of rain slap my face.
A cloudless sky in springtime.
A crow flaps overhead.
All becomes clear.
That was not rain.

Let's Take a Break

I want to go on holiday
Where the sky is blue.
I want to be in paradise,
So I don't want to go with you.

The Plane of Evil

How I hate the aeroplane,
That terrible tubular
Prison of pain.

The seat's too small
No legroom at all
And the trolley has missed me again.

The Amazon Basin

The sickness spreads.
I am not well.
A fever burns.
There's a funny smell.

My stomach lining
Is in a bowl,
And my bowels
Have lost control.

My hands are shaking.
I can barely see.
Jungle holidays
Are not for me.

English Seaside Break

Off they trot,
A nasty lot.
They're after a fight.
Its Friday night.

An easy trip
And the bed's for free.
A weekend stay
In A&E.

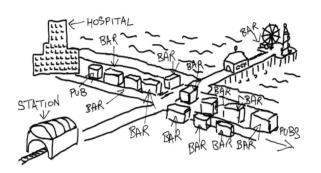

Coming to Mummy

You can hear my little feet
Padding to your door.
"Come in", you cry, "my little boy,
Don't worry anymore."

I can hear you in the dark.
"Mummy's here to hold you tight."
You can see me running now.
You've put on the light.

You start to scream as I skip in.
My little feet go pitter-pat.
I am not your bouncing baby boy.
I am a giant rat.

The First TV

Clever guy
Invents TV.
All his friends
Come to see.

He flicks the switch,
Then there're gone.
It was shit.
There was nothing on.

Just The Perfect Choice

Lovely flowers greet us
To take away the pain.
Poor old Auntie Florence.
We'll not see you again.

That Elton John song comes on.
The coffin trundles through the flame.
She died in a fire in her drafty house.
A fallen candle was to blame.

The Fairer Sex

Do you wash your bedding
Every single week?
Or maybe wait a month or two
Until you honk the reek?

Do you flip your mattress,
To fight the forming bowl?
Or maybe leave it where it is
And sleep deep in the hole?

You're a dirty dogman.
I know just what you're like.
Absolutely no chance, mate!
You can take a hike.

A Thing Called Love

They're walking in the park,
His arm around her shoulder.
She turns to smell the roses.
He gets a whole lot bolder.

He drops his arm down to her waist.
He does this stuff all day.
He has to hold on really tight
In case she runs away.

On Reflection

Looking in the mirror.
What is that I see?
A sunken sack of face flesh.
Fucking hell, it's me!

The Fun Run Out

Marathon On! On! On!
Terrible pain.
Too much strain.
I'm going lame
In both legs.

Had Enough Puff! Puff! Puff!
When will it end?
Round the next bend?
It'd be a godsend
Just to die.

I'm nearly Gone On! On! On!
Splitting brain-ache.
Must take a break.
For charity's sake,
I black out.

Who's A Silly Boy?

Waggy-tailed doggies,
Such furry balls of charm.
But they're not so cutesy-wootsy
With their teeth deep in your arm.

Waggy-tailed doggies,
The woggly ways they beg.
But they're not so sweet & funny
With their teeth deep in your leg.

Waggy-tailed doggies,
I loved them way too much!
Now my arm is one foot shorter
And I'm walking with a crutch.

One for the kids

The Wedding Party: Party I

A friend of the family.
An ominous phrase.
A person you won't like,
With peculiar ways

There's long chunks of silence
When you try to engage.
It's so painfully clear
You're not on the same page.

It's worse than the dentist.
Why's he still here?
You flounder in silence.
You gulp down your beer.

You've polished your pint off.
Thank god, you now think.
Make a run for the bar.
You need a drink.

The Wedding Party: Party II

A distant relation
Makes the heart sink.
You've just swapped discomforts
By getting a drink.

"It's been a long time!"
"Oh yes, it has been..."
And there's been good reason
For staying unseen.

This one's a talker
From a family of bores.
He twitches and scratches.
He's not one of yours.

Weave off into the crowd.
That's the way to shake free,
To escape from your brush
With a stray branch from the tree.

Note To Saddle Thief

I've got a bike,
Well, most of one.
The saddle was on.
Now it's gone.

You've got a bike
With my nice new seat.
Shove it up your arse.
It'll fit a treat.

The Waddling Walking, Scuttling Spider Story

A big black spider scuttles up the wall
I throw a shoe - this makes it fall.
Now it's coming straight at me,
And suddenly it's on my knee.
I hit it with a handy bottle,
So now when I walk,
I waddle.

I'm not feeling so good, either

I Made a Toilet Monster

It came from round the u-bend,
Far away from human glare.
It grew in bunged-up toilet paper
And tangled balls of shower hair.

With a massive fetid movement,
It wriggled down the drain.
Now it lurks around the neighborhood
And I must take the blame.

Screaming children run in horror.
Adults freeze with fear.
We all need tons of toilet roll
Every time it does appear.

Scaredy Cat Burglar

That's bad luck.
The window's stuck.
A quick escape is not to be.

They're home early
And he looks burly,
Could make a right mess out of me.

I'll be sneaky instead
And hide under the bed.
What a brilliant plan!

Lifting the sheet...
That's got me beat.
It's a bloody divan!

Sci-fi Movie Mystery

Down it floats, a gleaming ship,
Come to Earth on a cosmic trip.

A silver portal opens wide.
What brilliant beings live inside?

We wait to see this super-race,
Hi-tech travellers from outer space.

Out it stalks, a lizard-man-mutt
That cannot speak or wipe its own butt

Bold Vision

We need to have a meeting
To plan our future goal
And cover up the old plan
That's in the toilet bowl.

Let's make a bold new statement,
Support it with some books
And stick it in a document.
See how good that looks!

We're really going places now.
We're agile, fast and smart,
Selling up to move to Mexico
Before it falls apart.

Techie Heaven

I've made it in Tech
But I'm not done yet.
I'm going to live forever.

Going to upload my brain
Into the silicon cloud.
I'm so fucking clever.

When you are all dead,
I'll sit around in my chip
And err, hang out and do shit...
Or whatever...

Gut Issues

The sea was once free
From you and me.
Not land-locked in crap
Not caught in our trap,
It was better.

The sea is now sick.
It's drowning in junk,
Caught up in our game,
It's become just the same,
Only wetter.

The Final Room Review

I can't eat the food.
I can't take the drink.
The view is appalling.
There's no plug in the sink.

The light's too bright.
There's a load of beeping.
The bed is too soft.
It's no good for sleeping.

I've gone really cold
And it's all just a pain.
I can definitely say,
I'm not coming again.

That's It

Well, most of those were pretty good.
Yes, the pictures,
They were shit.
But I thought,
For the money,
I'd best pad it out a bit.

Shitflowers

9781399937863

BVRSH - #0004 - 151122 - C0 - 178/111/3 - PB - 9781399937863 - Matt Lamination